The

OUTHOUSE
READER

★ ★ ★

The
OUTHOUSE READER

TEXAS BIX BENDER & ROY ENGLISH

GIBBS SMITH
TO ENRICH AND INSPIRE HUMANKIND
Salt Lake City | Charleston | Santa Fe | Santa Barbara

First Edition
13 12 11 10 09   10 9 8 7 6 5 4 3 2 1

Published by
Gibbs Smith
P.O. Box 667
Layton, Utah 84041

Orders: 1.800.835.4993
www.gibbs-smith.com

Cover by Black Eye Design
Interiors by mGraphicDesign
Printed and bound in Canada
Gibbs Smith books are printed on either recycled, 100% post consumer waste, or FSC
certified papers.

Library of Congress Cataloging-in-Publication Data

Bender, Texas Bix, 1949–
  The outhouse reader / Texas Bix Bender and Roy English. — 1st ed.
    p. cm.
  ISBN-13: 978-1-4236-0468-6
  ISBN-10: 1-4236-0468-7
  1. American wit and humor. I. English, Roy, 1943– II. Title.
  PN6165.B45 2009
  818'.5402—dc22

                            2008043064

★ ★ ★

CONTENTS

• •

☞

★ ★ ★

As you read this, you are as one with the universe, because, rich or poor, powerful or weak, doctor or lawyer, or even president of the free world, everyone comes to this place to do the same thing that you do when you're here—read a good book.

* * *

GETTING ALONG

★ ★ ★

The shallower the stream,
the louder the

BABBLE.

[ENGLISH]

★ ★ ★

Strapping on a gun to protect yourself can get you **KILLED**.

(ENGLISH)

★ ★ ★

To know how country folk are doing, look at their barns, not their houses.

ENGLISH

★ ★ ★

Forgive your enemies;

it messes with their heads.

~English

* * *

"FRIEND"
is not always
all that friendly
a greeting.

(BENDER)

★ ★ ★

[It's downright annoying
to argue with a fella
who knows what he's
talking about.]

~English

★ ★ ★

Keeping your mouth shut and
being tactful might or might
not be the same thing.

*It depends
on your timing.*

[BENDER]

* * *

SMALL
MINDS
and **BIG**
MOUTHS
have a way
of hooking up.

(ENGLISH)

★ ★ ★

HOW LONG

"a few minutes" is
depends on
whether you're
in the bathroom
or waiting to get in.

BENDER

★ ★ ★

*There's no difference
between a
slim chance
and a fat chance.*

~Bender

★ ★ ★

You can't bury a fella just because he has been dead for years.

Forgiving your enemy doesn't guarantee he'll forgive you, but it's a start.

★ ★ ★

A persuasive man has more than ONE VOTE.

~English

★ ★ ★

A lot of people are smarter
than they look.

THEY GOTTA BE.

(BENDER)

★ ★ ★

DON'T WORRY

too much about what other people think about you. If they're giving you any thought at all, they're probably wondering what you think about them.

[BENDER]

★ ★ ★

You can't swat a fly that's sitting on the fly swatter.

~Bender

An ignorant fella is hell-bent on proving his limitations.

ENGLISH

* * *

Some folks
can stay longer in an
HOUR
than others can in a
MONTH.

(BENDER)

★ ★ ★

If you have to tell somebody you're just kidding, maybe you're not.

★ ★ ★

Know-it-alls are a
bother to those of us
who really
do know it all.

Do not shoot at the
horse; shoot at the
jackass ridin' it.

~Bender

★ ★ ★

—

ALWAYS

try to make folks happy, even
if that means going out of your
way to avoid them.

[BENDER]

★ ★ ★

One man's
sacred cow
is another's
Big Mac.

BENDER

★ ★ ★

---

*There are two
kinds of people in this
old world: those who
believe there are two
kinds of people,
and those who know*
better.

(BENDER)

★ ★ ★

[If you get all
wrapped up in yourself,
you'll find you make
a pretty small package.]

BENDER

Even the poorest cow has a leather coat.

(BENDER)

* * *

There may come a day
when the cow and the lion
will lie down together,

*but the cow won't
get much sleep.*

BENDER

★ ★ ★

Never feel too guilty over unkind thoughts about someone you love. It's for sure they've thought much worse things about you.

~Bender

★ ★ ★

---

*If you get to
thinkin' you're
a person of
some influence,
try orderin'
somebody else's*

DOG

around.

BENDER

★ ★ ★

Telling a man
to go to hell
and making
him do it
are two entirely
different
propositions.

(BENDER)

* * *

CONTROL
your generosity
when you're dealing with a
CHRONIC
BORROWER.

[BENDER]

NO TREE

is too big for a short dog to lift his leg on.

~Bender

★ ★ ★

*It's best to keep
your troubles pretty
much to yourself,
'cause half the people
you'd tell 'em to
won't give a damn,
and the other half
will be glad to
hear you've got 'em.*

BENDER

★ ★ ★

You cannot improve somebody's part by combing his head with a six-shooter.

It's hard to keep a secret around the campfire after a hearty meal of pinto whistleberries.

[BENDER]

★ ★ ★

A TRUE FRIEND—

if he can't get you out of jail,
will get in there with you.

ENGLISH

★ ★ ★

Country folks
laugh when you laugh,
cry when you cry,
know when you're sick,
and care when you die.

**Country fences need to
be horse high, pig tight,
and bull strong.**

(ENGLISH)

* * *

Don't loan money to a friend.

GIVE IT TO HIM.

You'll have a better chance
of being repaid.

(ENGLISH)

★ ★ ★

**Good fences
make good
neighbors—
especially when
your neighbor
is a donkey.**

~English

★ ★ ★

OLD FRIENDS

*started out as
new acquaintances.*

ENGLISH

* * *

WORK & SQUARE
DEALING

★ ★ ★

[

Country folks
will help a fella
who's down on his luck,
but they got no patience
with freeloaders.

~English

]

46

★ ★ ★

If you run with hounds, expect to get FLEAS.

(ENGLISH)

* * *

It's easy to win at Solitaire:
just shoot all the witnesses.
(BENDER)

---

*It's easier to patch
a broken mirror than
a reputation.*
[ENGLISH]

★ ★ ★

The lazy call the skillful
"LUCKY."

ENGLISH

★ ★ ★

Letting the cat
outta the bag
is a whole lot
easier than
putting it
back.

(BENDER)

★ ★ ★

Forget about justice.

Just do what's right.

~English

★ ★ ★

When somebody says
they're with you 110%,

*don't expect 'em
to be very good at math.*

[BENDER]

* * *

The surest
way to make
something
less great is to

EXAGGERATE

how great it is.

BENDER

★ ★ ★

*Figure out
what you stand for—
and what you won't.*

(ENGLISH)

* * *

Forget
WHO'S
right;
remember
WHAT'S
right.

ENGLISH

* * *

Your ways teach more than your words.

[ENGLISH]

It's not a miracle
if you find an orange
under an apple tree;
something ain't right.

BENDER

★ ★ ★

CROOKED
posts make
CROOKED
fences.

~English

★ ★ ★

Someone who tells you how honest he is may be trying to convince himself.

ENGLISH

A liar is just a lazy thief.

[ENGLISH]

The truth is simple—HARD but simple.

~English

★ ★ ★

Hoot owls and
bankers sleep with
one eye open.

(ENGLISH)

Money talks
but it don't always
make sense.

[BENDER]

★ ★ ★

THERE ARE
[NO]
friendly
ALLIGATORS.

~Bender

★ ★ ★

For rusty joints, try a little elbow grease.

ENGLISH

* * *

When a fella is
late for work, he
should do the
right thing and
leave work early
to make up for it.

(ENGLISH)

When you see a turtle sittin' on a fence post, you may not know how it got there, but you can be darn sure it had

HELP.

[BENDER]

★ ★ ★

NEVER
work for an outfit
you don't believe in.

~English

★ ★ ★

---

*When you're pickin'
a workin' horse, look for
one named Screwtail,
Stump Sucker, Rat's Ass,
Pearly Gates, Liver Pill,
or Darlin' Jill.
Leave the Champions
and Silvers for
the show ring.*

BENDER

★ ★ ★

Make yourself useful.

*If you can't weave a blanket,
mend a sock.*

[ENGLISH]

★ ★ ★

HE WHO HESITATES IS BOSSED.

(BENDER)

★ ★ ★

---

*A pennyweight
of doing is
worth more
than a
pound of*
PROMISING.

~English

★ ★ ★

Never underestimate yourself; there's always somebody around to do it for you.

BENDER

★ ★ ★

Gettin' up a lynch party is not

GROUP
THERAPY.

~Bender

★ ★ ★

*If you can keep your head
while all about you
are losing theirs,
you obviously don't
understand the situation.*

BENDER

★ ★ ★

When the herd
turns on you
and you're
forced to
run for it,
try to look like
you're leading
the charge.

(BENDER)

★ ★ ★

Don't get mad at somebody who knows more than you do.

It ain't their fault.

★ ★ ★

When you throw your weight around, be ready to have it thrown around by **SOMEBODY ELSE.**

~Bender

★ ★ ★

You don't have to step
in a cow pie to know what
shit smells like.

(BENDER)

★ ★ ★

BUILDING CHARACTER

* * *

A few rodeos don't make a **COWBOY**.

[ENGLISH]

★ ★ ★

*Being right all the time
doesn't gain a fellow much.*

(ENGLISH)

★ ★ ★

Dead right or dead wrong,

DEAD IS DEAD

~English

★ ★ ★

When you're green,
you grow;
when you think
you're ripe,
you get rotten.

★ ★ ★

Folks don't change;
They just get more so.
[ENGLISH]

★ ★ ★

The best sermons are LIVED, not preached.

(ENGLISH)

★ ★ ★

STAND FOR SOMETHING

or fall for everything.

~Bender

★ ★ ★

A fella who is too quick with an apology likely screws up a lot.

The sun does not rise to hear the ROOSTER.

[BENDER]

★ ★ ★

[
Some folks have
twenty years
of experience;
others have
one year
of experience
twenty times.

(ENGLISH)
]

★ ★ ★

Keep your
TEMPER;
nobody else
wants it.
~Bender

★ ★ ★

Some fellas have more wishbone than backbone.

Don't take too much pride
in being a good loser.

ENGLISH

* * *

Wisdom

is mostly learning to pace yourself.

[ENGLISH]

★ ★ ★

*Developing character
or throwing a steer
involves a struggle.*

(ENGLISH)

* * *

A wise man is quick to

LISTEN

and slow to

SPEAK.

ENGLISH

* * *

[**A person must meet fear to know courage.**]

~English

★ ★ ★

Feeling
sorry
for
yourself
is a
lonely
ride.

[ENGLISH]

★ ★ ★

No matter how big you think your

PUMPKIN

is, someone else has a bigger one.

(BENDER)

★ ★ ★

In old age, few regret
the **RISKS** they took.

~English

It's downright irritating
to be wrong when you're so
darned sure you're right.

BENDER

★ ★ ★

---

*If you're ridin' a high horse,
there ain't no way to get down
off it gracefully.*

Advice is like a pot of chili:
You should try a little of it
yourself before you
give anybody else a taste.

[BENDER]

★ ★ ★

A FELLA WHO IS **WISHY** ON ONE SIDE IS LIKELY **WASHY** ON THE OTHER.

(ENGLISH)

★ ★ ★

A steady
man
changes
without
CHANGING.

★ ★ ★

NEVER MISS A GOOD CHANCE TO SHUT [UP.]

(BENDER)

★ ★ ★

Horse races
are often won by a
nose—and a heart.

[ENGLISH]

SOUR GRAPES

make bitter wine.

(ENGLISH)

★ ★ ★

*Never lay an angry hand
on a kid or an animal;
it just ain't helpful.*

~**English**

★ ★ ★

If you don't
expect much,
you ain't
gonna
get much.

BENDER

★ ★ ★

OPPORTUNITY MAY KNOCK JUST ONCE,

but temptation is a frequent visitor.

[BENDER]

★ ★ ★

A horse is only as good as the man in the saddle.

(ENGLISH)

* * *

WANTS and NEEDS are two different things.

~English

★ ★ ★

There's no use for a man
who owns a dog
to do the barking himself.

BENDER

You can tell a lot
about a man
by how he shakes hands.

[ENGLISH]

★ ★ ★

Avoid flasharity,
foofaraw, and
fumadiddle
in dress, speech,
and conduct.
**Leave the peacocking
for the peacocks.**

(BENDER)

* * *

Even fools are

WISE

when silent.

~English

★ ★ ★

Anyone who yells
at a kid to prove who's
in control just did.

~English

★ ★ ★

A mule can't help it if his daddy is a jackass.

ENGLISH

★ ★ ★

In its mama's eyes, every sparrow is an

EAGLE.

[ENGLISH]

★ ★ ★

It takes more than having kids to be a DADDY.

(ENGLISH)

★ ★ ★

You're only young
for a while,
but you can be

childish

all your life.

~Bender

* * *

You can catch more flies with honey than with vinegar,

assuming you want to catch flies.

ENGLISH

★ ★ ★

You
can't
UNSAY
a cruel
thing.

[ENGLISH]

★ ★ ★

Every mama knows there is
greater joy in loving
than in being loved.

Roping and
good manners
take practice.

~**English**

* * *

EXPRESS YOURSELF KINDLY. BEING HONEST DOESN'T MEAN BEING CRUEL.

ENGLISH

* * *

**Don't take your boots off
under the table.
You don't want to compete
with the bouquet of the wine.**

[BENDER]

★ ★ ★

Eating with
your fingers is okay
if there are no
forks, spoons, or
knives around.
But eating with
someone else's
fingers is
almost **never**
good etiquette.

(BENDER)

★ ★ ★

---

*Farts are not
considered good dinner
conversation.*

Never ask a man
the size of his spread.

BENDER

★ ★ ★

Always say
"**PLEASE**"
when you tell
somebody to
SHUT UP.

~Bender

★ ★ ★

Slurping, burping, and gulping are only okay when you're alone with your dog. Same goes for any kind of licking.

`BENDER`

★ ★ ★

MUSINGS & AMUSING

★ ★ ★

When you doubt
God's sense of humor,
just look at
a woodpecker.

★ ★ ★

Regardless who won the race, I'd **RATHER** be a rabbit than a turtle.

(ENGLISH)

★ ★ ★

There is a lot to be said for

PATIENCE.

In time, even an egg will walk.

~Bender

★ ★ ★

A bird
in the hand
can be a
tad messy.

ENGLISH

★ ★ ★

Early to bed and
early to rise will
pretty much shut down
the domino game.

ENGLISH

★ ★ ★

"One of these days" is "none of these days."

[BENDER]

★ ★ ★

**The bull at
the front
of the herd
has the**

BEST VIEW.

(ENGLISH)

★ ★ ★

Life is not
about how
fast you run
or how high
you climb,
but how
well you
BOUNCE.

~English

* * *

We're all
one of a kind,

just like everybody else.

BENDER

★ ★ ★

If it ain't broke,
chances are it will be.
[ENGLISH]

* * *

A good cup of coffee
is the first
stirring event of the day.
(BENDER)

---

*You can't blame a worm for
not wanting to go fishing.*

~English

A SINGLE BROKEN HEART IS SAD.

A million broken hearts is a hit country song.

BENDER

A three-pound cat can
eat a four-pound fish.

[ENGLISH]

★ ★ ★

{ If athletes
get athlete's foot,
do astronauts
get missile toe? }
~Bender

The world
could use
a good
worrywart
remover.

(ENGLISH)

Oh, what tangled webs we weave
when first we practice to

BELIEVE.

~Bender

* * *

Life is like juggling pitchforks:
EVERYONE
knows when you mess up.

ENGLISH

★ ★ ★

If you
expect to be
surprised and
you're not,
that's still a
surprise.

[BENDER]

★ ★ ★

[*A cat that
licks its paw
may be scratching
its tongue.*]

(ENGLISH)

★ ★ ★

There are bugs from which you **cower**,
There are bugs you squeeze with **ease**,
There are bugs that bugs **devour**,
There are bugs that bite your **knees**,
There are bugs you hate with **passion**,
There are bugs at which you **scoff**,
But the bugs that eat your **flowers**
Are the bugs that **tick you off**.

[BENDER]

★ ★ ★

The best way to set a record
is to be a good ways off from
any tape measures, scales, or
witnesses.

(BENDER)

★ ★ ★

UNDERSTANDING THE SEXES

(Advice for Women & Men)

★ ★ ★

The transition from **boyhood** to **manhood** has very little to do with whiskers.

[ENGLISH]

Most men would rather mow a forty-acre pasture than a half-acre yard.

(ENGLISH)

149

★ ★ ★

DON'T LET A FOOL KISS YOU, OR A KISS FOOL YOU.

~Bender

★ ★ ★

The only time a woman can easily CHANGE a man is when he's a baby.

BENDER

★ ★ ★

A rooster does the crowing
while the hen does the work.

[ENGLISH]

* * *

Some women
think the
best way to
tell a good
watermelon
or a good man
is to give 'em
a good

THUMP.

(BENDER)

Women don't make
fools out of men; **they just
give 'em the opportunity**.

~Bender

* * *

When you go fishing for compliments, make sure you're using the RIGHT BAIT.

BENDER

★ ★ ★

When somebody
commences to
[flatterin' you,]
there's generally
more up their
sleeve than
just an arm.

~Bender

★ ★ ★

*If you're fixin' to get
yourself a good stallion,
don't go lookin' in
the donkey corral.*

[BENDER]

* * *

GIVE A MAN
A FREE HAND

and he'll run it all over you.

(MAE WEST)

★ ★ ★

Never comment on a woman's pregnancy unless you know for sure she is.

It's disturbing when a fella discovers that **his new bride snores like an Evinrude.**

ENGLISH

★ ★ ★

SOME PEOPLE
have no trouble separating the men from the boys.

These people are called women.

~Bender

★ ★ ★

Once her
broken heart
mends,
a woman
usually
feels like
a new man.

[BENDER]

★ ★ ★

If a woman can't make you miserable, she can't make you HAPPY

(BENDER)

* * *

If a man thinks
that a woman
who can dog steers,
ride broncs,
and rope the wind
is too much
for him,
**he's probably
right**.

BENDER

★ ★ ★

WHEN A MAN LOVES A WOMAN, HE CAN MAKE HER DO

anything she wants to.

[BENDER]

* * *

WINNING & LOSING
AT LOVE

★ ★ ★

It's
AWKWARD
when the
bride
thinks the
best man
really is.

[ENGLISH]

★ ★ ★

WHERE I COME FROM, HOOKING UP WITH A SPOUSE AIN'T NO *catch and release sport.*

(ENGLISH)

★ ★ ★

When you fall in love, you'll just know it. Same is true of measles and hemorrhoids.

~English

★ ★ ★

LOVE IS BLIND,

but marriage is a real eye-opener.

BENDER

★ ★ ★

Stumbling over the truth can break a heart.

[ENGLISH]

★ ★ ★

[
Goin' to bed mad
ain't no fun,
but it's better
than fightin' all night.
(ENGLISH)
]

★ ★ ★

The ties of
marriage are not
SLIPKNOTS.

~Bender

★ ★ ★

Two can live
as cheaply as one
if one don't eat.

Better to have loved
and lost than to
marry a dairy farmer.

ENGLISH

★ ★ ★

Pullin' your hair out over a broken heart will only make you **BALD**.

[BENDER]

★ ★ ★

---

*A young girl needs
something to love
when she is too old for dolls
and too young for boys.*

A horse is good.

(ENGLISH)

175

*It's a lot cheaper
to borrow money than
to marry for it.*

~Bender

★ ★ ★

COURTSHIP IS DANCING IN THE MOONLIGHT.

Marriage is washing socks.

ENGLISH

★ ★ ★

When a man
asks a woman
to share his lot,
**she has a
right to know
how big it is.**

[BENDER]

* * *

DIVORCE
changes the tire;

MARRIAGE
fixes the flat.

(ENGLISH)

★ ★ ★

Folks who expect to live happily ever after had best tend to it DAILY.

~English

★ ★ ★

Forbidden love

is a cactus bloom.

ENGLISH

* * *

A wedding ring
should cut off
the wearer's
circulation.

[BENDER]

* * *

For a happy marriage,
view your mate through a
**telescope, not a
microscope.**

(ENGLISH)

RESPECT

is love in work clothes.

~English

★ ★ ★

A heart
knows
things
a head
never
will.

ENGLISH

★ ★ ★

[Love is a castle
built of sand, and
sooner or later
the tide comes in.]

BENDER

★ ★ ★

Love is the delusion
that one idiot
differs from another.
(BENDER)

Most people fall in love in light so dim they wouldn't buy a suit in it.

~Maurice Chevalier

★ ★ ★

LOVE

**is a big, bright
blue balloon
in a world of**

STRAIGHT PINS.

[BENDER]

Let us be happy while we may
and seize love with laughter;
I'll be true as long as you,
but not for a moment after.

(BENDER)

★ ★ ★

. . . .

Love is affected by money
only up to a certain point—
a decimal point.

~Bender

. . . .

Politics doesn't make
strange bedfellows—
marriage does.

~Groucho Marx

. . . .

★ ★ ★

LOVE MAY
BE A BARGAIN,
but as in any bargain,
somebody always gets the
SHORT END OF
THE STICK.

BENDER

★ ★ ★

*You go into love blind
and come out
with 20/20 vision.*

[BENDER]

★ ★ ★

LOVE
is not
a word;
it's a sentence.

(BENDER)

★ ★ ★

Falling in love
is like buying something
on impulse: it looks great
when you pick it out,
but when you bring it home
**it just doesn't go
with anything.**

~Bender

* * *

OBSERVATIONS AND ODD FACTS

★ ★ ★

There are
hundreds of uses
for cowhide,
but the
most important
one is to
**hold the cow
together**.
[BENDER]

★ ★ ★

*A cow pony can't do
what a helicopter can,
and vice versa.*

**When diesel went to
$4 a gallon, I sold my tractor
and bought a mule. Then mule
feed went to $20 a bag.**

(ENGLISH)

I'm convinced that a warm supper
and a good night's sleep
is often the difference
between a hero and a coward
the next day.

~Lord Chesterfield

★ ★ ★

ONE BOY IS SOME HELP.
TWO BOYS ARE LESS HELP.
THREE BOYS AIN'T NO
HELP AT ALL.

ENGLISH

★ ★ ★

Firewood warms you twice:
WHEN YOU CUT IT,
WHEN YOU BURN IT.

[ENGLISH]

* * *

If you can't
rope a fence post,

CHANCES ARE

you'll miss roping
a wild heifer
from the
back of a
galloping pony.

(ENGLISH)

★ ★ ★

There's only a nickel's
difference between a
fella who works and one
who don't, and the one
who don't has the nickel.

~English

★ ★ ★

What you don't know **may not hurt you, but it can make you stupid.**

BENDER

★ ★ ★

Better to be **over** the hill

than under it.

[ENGLISH]

★ ★ ★

· · · · · · · · · · · · · · · · · · ·

Most things get better.
In fact, most things get better
by the next morning.

· · · · · · · · · · · · · · · · · · ·

Lightning is five times
hotter than the
surface of the sun.

· · · · · · · · · · · · · · · · · · ·

(BENDER)

★ ★ ★

A bumblebee is faster than a John Deere tractor.

[ENGLISH]

Remember that food artfully arranged has had somebody's fingers **ALL OVER IT.**

BENDER

★ ★ ★

{ Man is the
only critter
who feels the need
to label things
as flowers or weeds. }

~English

FACTS THAT
make no sense

Months that begin on a Sunday
will always have a Friday the 13th.

•

A cockroach can live several weeks
with its head cut off.

•

Worms taste like fried bacon.

•

It's against the law to have a
pet dog in Iceland.

•

Slugs have four noses.

★ ★ ★

FACTS THAT
do make sense

Elephants can't jump.

•

Women blink almost
twice as often as men.

•

An ostrich's eye is larger
than it's brain.

•

You can't kill yourself by
holding your breath.

(BENDER)

★ ★ ★

Country folks know a lot of stuff that ain't wrote down nowhere.

It's hard to plant a seedless grape.

~**English**

* * *

The sweetest peaches are just out of REACH.

ENGLISH

★ ★ ★

Less is more, but so is more.

[BENDER]

★ ★ ★

• •

Some city folks
think a square meal
is a sandwich.

• •

There are lots of
country jobs,
but few positions.

• •

(ENGLISH)

★ ★ ★

ABOUT HALF
YOUR TROUBLES
COME FROM
WANTING
YOUR WAY;
THE OTHER HALF
COME FROM
GETTIN' IT.

~Bender

* * *

Cream rises to the top,
but so does
some other crud.

Doing the Lord's work
doesn't pay much, but there's
a fine retirement plan.

★ ★ ★

BELIEVING IN SOMETHING MAKES IT POSSIBLE, NOT EASY.

[ENGLISH]

Most shortcuts are
DEAD ENDS.

(ENGLISH)

* * *

Hope is the
seed stock of

HAPPINESS.

~English

★ ★ ★

THE STRAIGHT POOP ON THE
John AND THE Crapper

Bathroom historians believe that it all began in England in 1596, when Sir John Harrington invented a really noisy valve that would allow a person sitting on the toilet to pull a chain and release water from an overhead water closet, thereby flushing the toilet. Sir John famously recommended that you flush at least twice a day. Some referred to his new invention as "going to the Harrington." He didn't like that one bit. After all, he was the godson of Queen Elizabeth I. So, he was very happy when people shortened it to his first name and called it going to "the John."

Then in 1819 a fellow countryman named Albert Giblin patented the "Silent Valve" for water closets. A lot of good it did him. Mr. Thomas Crapper employed Mr. Giblin at his plumbing business and wrangled the patent away from him. Maybe it was all for the best: Mr. Giblin's name is not slang for anything, but Mr. Crapper's name hit the fan, so to speak.

• • • • • • • • • • • • • • • • • • • (BENDER)

A FEW WORDS—MAYBE TOO FEW
On Toilet Paper
(NOT LITERALLY, OF COURSE)

BEFORE TOILET PAPER

Wealthy Romans used wool and sponges soaked in salt water.

•

Knights of the Round Table and others in the Middle Ages used hayballs on a scraper.

•

Early Americans used rags, newspapers, catalog pages, corncobs, and leaves.

•

In 1890, the Scott Paper Company came out with the first toilet paper on a roll. But they didn't want their name to become slang for anything, so they sold it in a plain brown wrapper. Merchants began to put their own name on it, and it became the first Store Brand—which many now use as a synonym for crap.

•

433 million miles of toilet paper are used every year in the USA.

The first toilet paper was produced in China in 1391 by the Bureau of Imperial Supplies for use by the emperor. Each sheet was exactly 2 x 3 feet. The emperor was the **BIG** man in China.

•

In 1857, in New York City, Joseph Gayetty began selling the first commercially available toilet paper. He called it "Therapeutic Paper." It came in individual 4-x-4-inch sheets and each one had his full name imprinted on it. It is amazing that his name is not associated with any slang words connected to what it was used for. Probably because no one knew what "therapeutic paper" was for and those that did weren't telling.

•

The average roll of toilet paper lasts 5 days in the average American household, unless it is the household of the average politician, who we all know is full of . . .

•

53% of people put the toilet paper on the roller to come out over the top. 47% of people put the toilet paper on the roller to come out underneath. Many gas stations don't put it on the roller at all.

•

In Japan they have toilets that wash, rinse, and blow dry. Then, after you put the lid down, they flush.

[BENDER]

★ ★ ★

ODD
Bathroom Facts

Only 46 percent of men
say they put the seat down;
yet 85 percent of women
admit to having fallen in the toilet
because the seat was up.

•

An unseen six-foot-high
spray of bacteria
spreads across a bathroom
every time the toilet is flushed
with the lid up.

BENDER

★ ★ ★

JUST FOR LAUGHS

★ ★ ★

[Don't whistle the
national anthem
'round the outhouse.]

ENGLISH

★ ★ ★

Considering everything,

I should feel guiltier than I do.

[ENGLISH]

★ ★ ★

When being chased by a bear,
run downhill.
You speed up, he slows down.

• • •

(Please let us know if this works.)

~English

★ ★ ★

*May your
life be like
a roll of
toilet paper:*

long and
useful.

~old elementary school saying

* * *

The only thing worse than
a lawn mower that won't start
is one that will.

Some folks
have to snore in
self-defense.

(ENGLISH)

★ ★ ★

Riddle:
What does it mean when
a country preacher
looks at his watch?

Answer:
It don't mean nothin'.

[ENGLISH]

★ ★ ★

Grave marker in a country cemetery:

I told y'all I was sick.
(ENGLISH)

★ ★ ★

IN TEXAS, A BURGLAR WAS recently fined 50 cents to pay for the bullet police shot him with when they caught him. When no one in the courtroom could make change for his dollar, they shot him again and **CALLED IT EVEN.**

~Bender

★ ★ ★

YEARS AGO,

**American Indians
tied small pine trees
to their feet
and invented
what we now call**

(a) Shoe trees

(b) Snowshoes

(c) Big Foot

BENDER

★ ★ ★

Eat beans;
they make you astute.

[BENDER]

★ ★ ★

★ ★ ★

For the third day in a row, firemen were called to extinguish a blaze at the home of Mr. and Mrs. Howard Endorf. All the calls to the fire department have occurred between the hours of six and seven in the morning. When asked about this, Mister Endorf said, "Well, that's when I get up and put the water on for a cup of instant coffee." Mrs. Endorf normally makes Mr. Endorf's coffee, but she has been out of town for three days now, visiting her sister.

• • • • • • • • • • • • (BENDER)

★ ★ ★

A tragic event was narrowly averted this morning when Mrs. Vernice Mendenhall thought she had slept with a bear. It seems her husband was on vacation and had not shaven or bathed for six days. Around four in the morning, Mrs. Mendenhall was awakened by what she believed to be the threatening growl of a grizzly bear. In reality, it was her snoring husband. But in the dim glow from a nightlight, her husband's grizzled features convinced her that a bear had crept into her bed during the night, eaten her husband, and taken his place. With great courage and daring, she leapt from the bed, grabbed her husband's fully loaded twelve-gauge shotgun and let go with both barrels. Fortunately for Mr. Mendenhall, the recoil from the heavy blast caused her to shoot high and blow out the wall behind the bed. It was reported that Mr. Mendenhall slept though the whole thing. The noise of carpenters repairing the wall eventually roused him.

~Bender

★ ★ ★

The best way to
cook any part of a
rangy ol' longhorn is to
toss it in a pot with a
horseshoe, and when the
horseshoe is soft and tender,
you can eat the beef.

BENDER

★ ★ ★

A Texas breakfast is a two-pound hunk of steak, a quart of whiskey, and a hound dog. If you're wondering why you need the dog—well, somebody has to **EAT THE STEAK.**

[BENDER]

★ ★ ★

*Nature gave us all
something to fall back on,
and sooner or later we all*
land flat on it.

(BENDER)

* * *

SOUND
ADVICE

★ ★ ★

Even a horse thief
has a purpose in life.

Find
yours.

[ENGLISH]

★ ★ ★

[When leaving a
barroom brawl,
walk out backwards.]

(ENGLISH)

★ ★ ★

LIFE IS NOT A SHORTCUT.

~Bender

★ ★ ★

When you get a critter on the run, **DON'T STOP** to assess the situation.

ENGLISH

* * *

TIME

is the only
currency that
matters.

SPEND IT WELL.

[ENGLISH]

★ ★ ★

When a twister is coming,
don't mistake the
outhouse for the cellar.

(ENGLISH)

Horse sense comes
from a stable mind.

(BENDER)

★ ★ ★

Don't name a pig you plan to eat.

~English

It's not true that chewing gum can cure a cold, but it can plug a runny nose.

BENDER

* * *

Life is
SIMPLER
if you plow
around the
stumps.

[ENGLISH]

★ ★ ★

If at first you don't succeed, try raising rabbits.

Don't skinny dip with snappin' turtles.

(ENGLISH)

★ ★ ★

THINGS ARE NOT WHAT THEY SEEM TO BE, OR SO IT SEEMS.

~Bender

★ ★ ★

One in a row is a

good start.

BENDER

★ ★ ★

Don't sell your mule to buy a plow.

• • • • • • • • • • •

Don't go hunting with a fella named CHUG-A-LUG.

[ENGLISH]

★ ★ ★

Keep talking
to your kids,
{ **no matter what.** }

~English

* * *

Don't let so much reality into your life that there's no room left for **DREAMING**.

BENDER

★ ★ ★

Most of the things folks worry about NEVER HAPPEN.

[ENGLISH]

Nothing is impossible,

except peeing in a naked man's pocket.

(ENGLISH)

★ ★ ★

Don't smoke in the hay loft.

Don't stand behind
a coughing cow.

~English

★ ★ ★

It's possible to make a sound **argument** without making a lot of noise.

BENDER

★ ★ ★

[Don't rock back on a
three-legged stool.

~English]

* * *

Don't try to hold a barn cat against his will.

[ENGLISH]

* * *

Whatever
the
illness,
time
is the
best cure.

(ENGLISH)

★ ★ ★

FEED a cold, **STARVE**
a fever, **SOAK** a thorn,
AIR a wart.

~English

★ ★ ★

IT'S BEST TO STOP TALKING

once you've said all you know.

ENGLISH

* * *

Mount a horse
from the **left**.
Milk a cow
from the **right**.
Approach a mule
from the **front**,
a billy goat
from the **rear**.

[ENGLISH]

★ ★ ★

ADMIT YOUR
MISTAKES

[*but don't wallow in them.*]

~English

★ ★ ★

Work hard to be good,
not perfect.

(ENGLISH)

* * *

Living in
the past is
DANCING
with a
DEAD MAN.

ENGLISH

266

★ ★ ★

Forgive and **forget** the best you can.

~English

★ ★ ★

ADVICE

is no better than the one who gives it.

[ENGLISH]

Never sit a
barbwire fence naked.

~Bender

Be careful when
choosing heroes.

~English

★ ★ ★

If a woman spills her drink,
hand her a napkin
and let her do the patting.

(BENDER)

Cheap boots
are rarely
a bargain.

(ENGLISH)

PRAY FOR GOODNESS, NOT THINGS.

~English

★ ★ ★

WILD BILL HICKOCK'S SIX RULES TO AVOID BEING AMBUSHED:

1. Never come in through the front door.
2. Walk in the middle of the street and keep an eye on the alleyways.
3. Sleep with wadded-up newspapers scattered all around the bed. (Anybody sneaking in will crunch them and wake you up.)
4. Always have a gun within easy reach.
5. Shoot first and forget the questions.
6. Never sit with your back to a door or window.

On August 2, 1876, Wild Bill broke rule number 6. He was 39 years old and would never be 40. He was by then, according to some, more of a drinker than a gunfighter. Already half-drunk, according to witnesses, he entered Nuttall & Mann's Saloon in Deadwood, South Dakota, as the sun was going down. A poker game was under way, and the only open seat had its back to the front door and the bar. Wild Bill asked if any of the players would trade places with him and take that seat. None would. So, he sat down and they dealt him in. A short while later, Jack McCall, who Wild Bill had cleaned out in a game at the same table the night before, slipped up behind him and shot Hickock in the back of the head. Wild Bill was holding a pair of aces and eights, all clubs and spades—a hand that has ever since been called the "Dead Man's Hand."

[BENDER]